Departed Friends
"Good Grief"

Jacqui Hill Goudeau

Copyright © 2013 Jacquelyn Hill Goudeau

All rights reserved. No part of this publication may be reproduced, stored in a retrieval system, or transmitted in any form by means electronic, mechanical, photocopying, recording or otherwise, except or the inclusion of brief quotations in a review, without prior permission in writing from the publisher.

ISBN-13:
978-0989623315 (Jacquelyn Hill Goudeau)

ISBN-10:
0989623319

DEDICATION

JEHOVAH SHAMMAH (The Lord is there)

&

Joe L. Gunn and Mary E. Gunn, affectionately known as Mommy and DJ Thanks for the life lessons and for lives well lived. Truly an example for generations to come.

CONTENTS

"Even When I'm Hurting"
Introduction

1	When Nobody Understands	13
2	The Blame Game	19
3	Major Changes	27
4	Gaining Through Loss	33
5	Handling Holidays	39
6	When Children Mourn	45
7	Why Push for Healing?	51
8	How to be Healed	57
9	Healing Without Closure	61
10	When Unbelievers Die	69
11	Notable Deaths	75
12	It's Time!	81
13	Personal Notes	87
	A Final Thought	93
	Scripture Promises	95

Even When I'm Hurting

Jacqui Hill-Goudeau

Even when I'm hurting, with me Oh Lord, You'll be,
Ever present, ever loving, ever watching over me.
Even though I may be broken and feeling deep despair,
You will ever be beside me keeping me within Your care.
When death or life may shock me with pain I never knew,
My true and greatest comfort will come from time with You.
Though my heart is barely beating and breathing hard to do,
You are sending me great people with a heart to see me through.

At times anger engulfs me, and I don't know how to feel,
But Your word gently reminds me that one day I too will heal.
Guilt sometimes will show his face, he taunts my weary mind,
But if I keep Your focus, even then Your peace I'll find.

Through my loss I've not forgotten, as my loved ones went away,
Your goal is not me forgetting them as I heal from day to day.
But Your goal is that I remember You, even though I feel this pain,
By doing that I choose to love and learn to live again.

Lord, You are ever near, seeing me through every day.
Ever keeping, ever pulling, and ever coaching me along the way.
So even when I'm hurting, with me I know You'll be,
Ever present, ever loving, ever watching over me.

You will keep him in perfect peace, whose mind is stayed on You, because he trusts in You.
Isaiah 26:3

INTRODUCTION

Grief is a very real part of every person's life. Sometimes we can go through it really well, and other times we may just lose it. There are even times we think we won't be able to make it, but strength comes from somewhere and we survive. This booklet comes from a class entitled ***"Departed Friends–Good Grief."*** This book is simply a Christian's view based on God's word. It's to remind us of how God will help us through whatever we deal with in life. His word holds answers for us even in the midst of great pain. Throughout the year you may find someone who needs encouragement or you yourself may need it. There is hope for you and peace for your mind because you still have a future. God's plan is that you trust Him in all things and lean on Him even when you find it hard to stand.

When dealing with grief we will find the greatest opportunity to trust God. How we handle this area of life speaks to what we think about God. If God is the God of all comfort, that means He is able to comfort us, no matter what the issue, no matter how much it may hurt, or how much we don't understand. If He is the God of all comfort, then we have to trust Him to help us, even when it hurts so badly.

Normal Feelings and Responses:

Hopelessness   Loneliness

          Anger   Loss of appetite

Fear   Loss of drive for life

     Guilt   Restlessness

If you are experiencing any of these feelings, you have an answer in God. He is our hope. He is ever present. He will calm our fears and clear our conscience. He is the Giver of Life and knows everything. Sometimes we can only rest in the fact that the pain we are feeling now, He knew would come, but promised never to leave us in the midst of it.

Different kinds of death:

      Natural - old age

      Untimely - accidents, violence, tragic occurrences

      Innocent - children

      Suffering - lengthy illness

      Sudden - unknown situations

Regardless to what type of death you may be dealing with, God **is** the God of all comfort. He is willing and able to hold you up, to help you and to encourage you to continue to fulfill your purpose. **Allow Him to do it!**

 Take your time reading this booklet. Stop for a while if you need to, and allow God to make His promises real to you. Spend time in personal study with each chapter, and gain more strength than you ever had before.

Father God, Thank You for my brother or sister. Thank You for caring about them more than they can imagine right now. I thank You that You promised to be a comfort to Your people. You promised to never leave or forsake us. Touch this reader right now and let them feel Your tangible presence; encourage their hearts and minds and help them in this time. We thank You for being ever present to help in time of need. Meet their need right now. We give You glory for it. In Jesus' name.

Amen.

CHAPTER 1

WHEN NOBODY UNDERSTANDS

"You will find people who do not understand your grief. They look at your life and think you have so much to be thankful for and this is just one hard time in the midst of many blessings. Or they may even remind you, 'It could have been worse.'"

When Nobody Understands

Samuel 18:33 - *And the king was much moved, and went up to the chamber over the gate, and wept: and as he went, thus he said, O my son Absalom, my son, my son Absalom! Would God I had died for thee, O Absalom, my son, my son!*

David was a man who had many obstacles in life. Like us, he probably wished he could enjoy his family and live a long prosperous life. But life did not grant that to him. He found himself running from Saul, at war with his son, and facing the embarrassment and consequences of his own sin. But he remained a "man after God's own heart."

David's son, Absalom, was a serious threat to the king and was not thinking about his father as he tried to tear the kingdom from him, but he was nevertheless, David's son. When the word came that Absalom was dead, David responded as any parent would. He was torn and broken at the loss of his son. Many would wonder why he mourned so hard for a son who had caused him so much grief. But, no matter what you say, the loss of a child is still the loss of a child, no matter how that child behaved.

Grief can feel the same whether the person is taken from you suddenly, if you could see the day approaching, or whether you were close to them or not. Sometimes we can grieve harder for a relationship lost because we never gave ourselves to it and now it is too late. Don't feel like something is wrong with you just because you seem surprised by what was inevitable to others. Our faith can often confuse us when the answer to our prayer doesn't come like we thought. **After all truth faith can have us holding on until the very end.**

Many times in life you will find people who do not understand your grief. They look at your life and think you have so much to be thankful for and this is just one hard time in the midst of many blessings. Or, they may even remind you, "It could have been worse." Right now, all you may feel is how bad it is. It can't be compared to a possibility. This is your reality. In an attempt to help us handle grief, people often say and do the exact opposite of what we need.

WHAT TO SAY?

When a person is hurting from the death of a loved one, there is not much one can say to help. Sometimes just listening is best. We often feel obligated to say the right thing, but sometimes there is no right thing. If we aren't careful, we can end up saying all the wrong things and have an adverse effect on the person we are trying to help.

Here is a short list of what NOT to say!

- ❖ "You can have another child"- as if this one is insignificant...
- ❖ "They lived a full life"- how do you measure full?
- ❖ "You can marry again" -but this is the person I chose...
- ❖ "God wanted a rose from His garden"- isn't He the Creator?

- ❖ "It could be worse"- I know it can...
- ❖ "You'll get over it, just wait and see"- Get over what? Them?
- ❖ "You have lots of people who love you"- I just lost one.

Sometimes we try to say something that is useful, when really praying for the person is best. Your presence, even if silent, may mean more to some people than all the words you can muster up. If you are in a situation where no one seems to understand, know that God knows your hurt and your pain. He has been touched with the feelings of your infirmities, and has made a way of escape for you. Just continue to trust Him, and He will bring you through this hard time, with your right mind.

Father God, Thank You for knowing what I need even more than I do. Thank You for good people that can hear from You and be used to help and pray for me during this time. I accept that many may not know what to do, but thank You that their intentions are for me. Help me to accept and appreciate the acts of kindness that are meant to help me. Most of all, thank You for helping me to wake every morning and just breathe. In Jesus' name. Amen.

Notes

CHAPTER 2

THE BLAME GAME

"The hardest thing about blaming anyone for the death of a loved one is that it doesn't change anything."

The Blame Game

Are you blaming someone? If so, who?

The hardest thing about blaming anyone for the death of a loved one is that it doesn't change anything.

Blaming Yourself?

This is an easy out. If we blame ourselves we don't have to worry about getting an argument from anyone.

- ...Blaming yourself for not being there
- ...For not making them see a doctor sooner
- ...For not driving them to their destination
- ...For not making them stay home
- ...For not doing something

You can blame yourself all day, but it will still not change anything. Realize you are not God. You probably couldn't have changed anything, even if you tried. Release yourself!

Blaming Others?

Sometimes there is a legitimate reason why we blame others. They may have been involved or seemed to be passive in their actions to intervene. Or, they may just be a good target for now since nothing else makes sense.

- ❖ … Blaming the doctors and their staff
- ❖ …The person who drove the other car
- ❖ …Family members for not being there
- ❖ …The person responsible for injuries that led to death
- ❖ …Family members that show up after the fact

Sometimes blaming others seems like it will work. But after we vent our anger, we still have to deal with the fact that our loved one is gone. The energy we use blaming could be put into living, surviving our pain and helping our family do the same.

> **By releasing others, you release yourself to God so you can be healed.**

Blaming the Deceased?

Anger after the loss of a loved one can often turn into blaming them. Knowing they are gone and you don't want them to be, can sometimes cause you to respond by blaming them for leaving.

- ❖ ... They should have gone to the doctor.
- ❖ ... Not have been where they were.
- ❖ ... Could have gotten help.
- ❖ ... Promised to always be there.
- ❖ ... Cooperated with the doctors.
- ❖ ... They never listened.

When we blame the deceased, we also have to deal with the guilt of having those feelings. They are not here to argue the point with us. Nothing is more frustrating than arguing with someone who is not answering you. It is best to release it and allow God to heal us. It also allows us to have a better memory of our loved one if we are not continuing to hold anger towards them.

Blaming God?

As people of faith, this can mess us up. We cannot believe our God, who loves us, would allow us to feel the pain we feel. So we ask the questions:

Does God really love me?

- ❖ What have I done to deserve this hurt?
- ❖ Am I being punished?
- ❖ Why would God allow this to happen?
- ❖ I have prayed and fasted, why did God not answer?
- ❖ Is God real, or have I been deceived?

Many people are angry with God in the loss of a loved one. Many walk away and it takes major intervention to get them back to Him. God is all knowing, and He does answer prayer. Trying to understand some things would only drive us crazy. Some things we will never understand. That is why trusting Him becomes so important. Learn to trust Him with the unexplainable. Rely on the fact that God does love us and has everything in control is sometimes hard to do, but it is necessary. Many unbelievers feel this is a cop-out. It is our way of holding a crutch because we can't explain God's actions or lack of actions. But when you really know God, you realize He is Omniscient. He knows everything! I only know what I can sense, see or feel. But God will still work things together for good if I love Him and am called according to His purpose. God is bound by His word. Sometimes things happen in this life, and because we are the only creation with our own will, God has to LET us do whatever we are doing. He works around circumstances to bring about the best for us, but it is not always without casualties. Some outcomes are more our doing, not His. Trust that God really does love you and cares about everything that concerns you. Run to Him, not away from Him, and allow Him to work in your circumstance. He is waiting for you.

Conclusion

Blaming is never going to help you heal. It will only cause a root of bitterness to develop because of whoever you are blaming. The best thing to do is to talk to God. Get in His word and find peace. Try to answer the issues in your mind and press past the dark areas of "what if?" Grace is available to you to make it through hard days, so pull on God. He is the God of all Grace. He will empower you to accept what you cannot change.

Father God,

Thank You for Your word that is allowing me to release any hurt, bitterness or unforgiveness that I may be holding towards myself, others, my loved one or even You. I know that You hold life and no one else could change what has been done. But I thank You for making a way for me to receive healing and peace in my mind. I release every person I may be holding something against. I know my feelings require a process, but my heart's desire is to please You, so I make the decision to forgive and to release the blame I may be holding towards them. Thank You that my feelings line up to Your will as I choose to release it. Father, as never before, I trust You. I lean on You; I appreciate You. Thank You for allowing me to know Your comfort and forgiveness. Strengthen me to make it through this difficult time and I will remember to give You all the glory and honor. In Jesus' name. Amen.

Notes

CHAPTER 3

MAJOR CHANGES

"A great temptation when we lose someone, is to remove all reminders, clean up rooms, throw away or give away items they owned and hurry up to go on with our lives."

Major Changes

Don't make major changes during this time.

After Jesus' death, he appeared to his disciples and told them:

"Behold I send the promise of My Father upon you, but tarry in the city of Jerusalem until you are endued with power from on high." (Luke 24:49)

A great temptation when we lose someone is to remove all reminders, clean up rooms, throw away or give away items they owned and hurry up to go on with our lives. Maybe to convince friends that we are healing in a healthy way. Or maybe so they realize we are not in denial. This is not always the best thing to do. During emotional times, our reasoning may be off. Our ability to make good decisions may be blurred. I spoke to a woman from another culture and their practice is to not make major decisions or changes for one full year. This includes painting the house, selling it, changing furniture around, and dividing the estate and other things. That may seem like an extreme, especially since our culture requires deadlines for certain estate business and some larger families don't want to wait unnecessarily for dividing inheritance or handling business. So it may not be practical to hold on everything for a full year, but here is a short list of things that you may consider waiting to do during your early stage of grief.

Things you may need to hold off on:

- ❖ Unplanned job changes- quit jobs
- ❖ Relationship changes- divorce, marry or separate
- ❖ Living changes- move from the home
- ❖ Discard all their belongings, sell stuff, giveaway keepsakes
- ❖ Leave your church home
- ❖ Move out of town to start again

> **If you are not careful, you can end up extending your grieving period because you ran from the pain. If you make too many changes you may regret them later.**

How the opposite can be just as traumatic.

Not changing anything, not clearing out belongings, not changing their favorite room, refusing to love again or not allowing yourself to progress. We can end up living in fear that we will forget our loved ones, or that we may be hurt if we love again. Stay prayerful as you strive to keep an even balance in making changes in your life, your job, and your home. Sometimes you have to stay put until God empowers you to go on.

He will do it!

Father God,

You said in Your word, that "If any man lacks wisdom, he can ask of You." Father, I pray for wisdom in every area of my life. Thank You for giving me wisdom in my decisions, wisdom in how I deal with others, and wisdom in making changes in my life. During this time in my life, I choose to not be led by my feelings or emotions, but by You. You said in Your word that, "The steps of a good man are ordered by You." Father, thank You for ordering my steps. I choose to follow the path You lead me on. Thank You for helping me to not be led by my emotions or the emotions of others. Thank You for caring about every area of my life and for watching over me. I am open to the people You give me for my life. Help me identify those that are good for me and those that may be a hindrance. Help me celebrate the people that are still in my life as gifts from You. Father, I also thank You for my future that You hold. You know the plans You have for me. Help me to do my part in fulfilling them even if I don't know them. I trust You with my hope and my expected end. In Jesus' name. Amen.

Notes

CHAPTER 4

GAINING THROUGH LOSS

"Grief over any loss can have a positive effect if it brings us to the feet of the Savior"

Gaining in Loss

> "Blessed are those who mourn, for they shall be comforted" Matthew 5:4

Spiritual mourning: our grief, sorrow or sadness over our sins and our failures; lost relationship with God.

Natural mourning: our grief, sorrow or sadness over the loss of loved ones through death or broken relationships.

Romans 5: 2-5 "We rejoice in the hope of the glory of God. Not only so, but we also rejoice in our sufferings, because we know that suffering produces <u>perseverance</u>, perseverance, <u>character</u>; and character, <u>hope</u>. And hope does not disappoint us, because God has poured out His love into our hearts by the Holy Spirit, whom He has given us."

What can we gain in loss?

        Perseverance

        Character

        Hope

God is never wasteful. Even in our bad experiences, if we are open to Him, we can learn. Perseverance can be found in the heart of a loved one who is willing to go the extra mile for a loved one, when in their own life they seem passive. Character is built when you have to face various personalities in the midst of turmoil, but you hold it together for the sake of your loved one or God's namesake. Hope is found whenever you trust God. Faith and hope go together. Whenever you show faith in God, hope is always connected. It is the looking at what **else God will do, what He is able and willing to do** for us.

Grief calls for us to make changes in our lives that will either enrich or impoverish us. Here are some ways we can gain in loss:

- ❖ We can learn patience at a loved one's bedside
- ❖ We can change how we interact with others
- ❖ We can change how we treat our family
- ❖ We can change how we see life as a whole
- ❖ We can take time to enjoy little things in life
- ❖ We may spend more time with family and friends
- ❖ We can change how and how quickly we respond to God

We can become bitter or better! Choose better!

Father God, I will never be able to understand how You can take horrible circumstances and cause them to work out for my good. In some situations, I can't even imagine trying to see how, especially when I am hurting. But again, I choose to trust You. I choose to grow and be a better person in the midst of all of this. I choose to listen for Your direction so I can follow a path to healing. I just choose YOU. I ask that You will help me see You in all this. Help me not blame You, but see You – See Your hand in a way I never would have before. Help me to be a blessing to others as they see Your grace working in me.

Thank You for staying close by me through all of this. In all of this, I choose to trust You. In Jesus' name. Amen

Notes

CHAPTER 5

HANDLING HOLIDAYS

"Special days can be ruined before they even arrive if we are not ready for the blow that the loss of a loved one can bring"

Handling Holidays

Mother's Day, Father's Day, Grandparent's Day, Special Anniversaries, Birthdays, Christmas and Thanksgiving.

Holidays are times to reflect and come together with family and friends. Special days can be ruined before they even arrive if we are not ready for the blow that the loss of a loved one can bring. Some traditions are put on hold because of the memories it may bring. But you should ask yourself, "Why can't it still be done? Would my loved one want us to enjoy time with family and friends? Would I want my family to pull together on special days and remember me as they celebrate?" Take time to be around people who care about you. It will make your grieving time less isolated.

Some things to help:

- ❖ Talk to God early - don't wait for the holiday to come
- ❖ Prepare your mind (It may be festive)-don't take it personally
- ❖ Do something! Plan time based on your limitations
- ❖ Spend time with friends or family-plan ahead
- ❖ Make traditions fresh and make new ones
- ❖ Don't avoid speaking about your loved one, you may feel guilty later
- ❖ Remember, every year you will face holidays and special occasions

It is not a problem for others to enjoy the day, even if you have difficulty with it. No one is trying to make your day worse. Here is a bible example of how the Jews changed what the enemy intended for pain into joy:

Esther 9:22

"As on the day that the Jews got relief from their enemies, and as the month that had been turned for them from sorrow into gladness and from mourning into a holiday, that they should make them a day of feasting and gladness, days for sending choice portions to one another and gifts to the poor."

On a day that was supposed to bring pain and anguish for the Jews, they did something different: They made it a day of celebration!

If you are familiar with the story of Esther, you know that the Jews were sentenced to death. Because of Esther and the advice from her uncle, the plot of their enemy was thwarted. But they were still doomed to die based on the decree from the King. The only way the king could change it, was to issue another decree. His new decree enabled them to defend themselves. That was all. They were still at risk of being attacked. That never changed. But the ability to defend yourself, to fight for your right to live, will change everything. Every year after that fateful day, the Jews did something different. **They made it a day of celebration!** The King of Kings has enabled you to fight back in the midst of things that are meant to ruin your day!

This is the day the Lord has made and I will rejoice and be glad in it! ~Psalms 118:24

Sometimes we have to purpose how our day will go. We have to plan ahead of time to defeat the enemy who intends to keep us hurting and emotionally bankrupt.

What can you do?

- ❖ **Find someone to bless– adopt a brother or sister**
- ❖ **Take time to follow up on family and friends**
- ❖ **Start a scholarship in the name of your loved one**
- ❖ **Find family members who are hurting and bless them**

Many ministries have begun because of the death of a loved one. Crime prevention measures have been initiated because of a victim's family. Laws have been passed because of the fight for justice that someone went on to vindicate their loved one. Hospitals have been built in the name of patients that did not survive the very thing that their name now promotes education on. Scholarships in the area that a loved one had an interest, can grow into foundations that will bless others for years to come. What a legacy!

What can you do to remember your loved ones in a positive way? Put your energy into purpose! <u>Remembering is not all bad.</u>

Notes

CHAPTER 6

WHEN CHILDREN MOURN

"The age of a child may affect the grieving process."

When Children Mourn

Children mourn for the same reasons adults do.

- ❖ Loss of a parent, grandparent or family member
- ❖ Loss of a close friend or pet
- ❖ Loss of relationship– divorce or relocation
- ❖ National losses in the news

How Children Mourn:

Some children are obvious mourners, while others don't seem to respond or know what is going on. Some children may seem to be in denial. Sometimes grades can be affected; a child that did well in school may find themselves struggling to focus. A normally mild-mannered child may be found getting in fights. Some children have physical reactions like nausea or unexplained illness; some may begin to wet the bed or have nightmares. They may increase in sleeping or not be able to sleep at all. Some younger children may have a lot of questions that are difficult and almost impossible to answer. Somehow, we have to take care of our babies, even when we are hurting.

Common Mistakes Adults Make:

- Lying. Sometimes we don't know how to explain, so we fabricate something that "sounds" better
- We may forget and only focus on the adults involved
- We may think they are too young to understand
- We may insist the child talk about the loss
- We may not allow the child to talk about the loss
- Assuming the child's grieving process is abnormal
- Assuming the child's grief process is normal

Things to Help:

- Know your child!
- Keep a routine in the home– bed time, meals, etc.
- Allow the child to open up and talk when they need to
- Answer questions as truthfully as possible
- Use wisdom in attending or not attending services
- Graveside visits might confuse small children
- Teach children about death being a natural part of life early
- Help children to have a real relationship with God
- Use instructional books to help identify your child's needs

Note: If you are concerned about your youth or child, it is okay to seek help from your church or a professional counselor.

Father God,

Thank You for watching over our children, and for caring about all who may be affected by death. I pray that You will help us deal delicately with every area of each child's life. Help us not be so consumed with grief that we forget their little hearts may be broken as well. For all those who don't have an understanding, help them. For those who are dismayed, encourage them. For any child that does not know You or understand that death is a natural part of life, allow Your people to cover them with Your comfort and love. I pray that the children will not experience negative effects in their lives because of the losses they may encounter. Work it all out for them. Let them hold onto Your hand as they go into their future, and give them peace in the midst of every storm. Thank You for always caring for our children. In Jesus' name. Amen.

Notes

CHAPTER 7

WHY PUSH FOR HEALING?

"God is not finished with you yet"

Push For Healing

Being confident of this very thing, that He who has begun a good work in you will perform it until the day of Jesus Christ.

Philippians 1:6

We have a promise that God will continue working in us. We have to make a commitment that we will allow Him to do it.

God is not finished with you yet!

In 2 Samuel, David confused his servants by how he grieved for the child that he lost with Bathsheba. He mourned and wept and refused to eat until he found that the child was dead. They were afraid to tell him the child was dead, but were really confused when, **"... he arose from the earth, washed anointed himself and changed his apparel and came into the house of the Lord and worshipped; then he came to his own house and when he required, they set bread before him and he did eat."**

2 Samuel 12:20

His servants asked him about his actions and he answered them by saying: *"While the child was yet alive, I fasted and wept: for I said who can tell whether God will be gracious to me that the child may live? But now he is dead, why should I fast, can I bring him back again? I shall go to him, but he shall not return to me."* And David comforted Bathsheba his wife and went into her and lay with her, and she bore a son, and he called his name Solomon; and the Lord loved him.

So why should you push for healing?

Because there is still a **Solomon** in you! There is still a promise, a purpose, a gift that God has in you. Something He plans to use, something He loves. We push for our healing because someone needs the gift in us. What God has put in you could change the world. Push for your healing!!

Rise and Be Healed!

Father,

Thank You that I still have a hope and a future. I still have a purpose and You still have a plan for my life. Help me to push past what I see and how I feel so I can fulfill all that You have for me. I thank You that You have not cast me away. Thank You for allowing me time to heal and for allowing me time to deal with my hurt. But Father, I realize You have more for me, more in me, and Your plan is that it comes forth. I am ready now to hear and obey. Father redeem the time I have lost, by causing my works for You to multiply! Touch more than I thought, encourage more than I can imagine, and save more than I ever thought possible. Thank You for continuing the work You began in me. In Jesus' name. Amen.

Notes

CHAPTER 8

HOW TO BE HEALED

"Do you want to be made well?"

How to Be Healed

When Jesus saw him lying there and knew that he already had been in that condition a long time, He said to him: "Do you want to be made well?" John 5:6.

Believe it or not, there are similarities between physical and emotional healing. In this story, Jesus comes across a man who has been sick for 38 years. When Jesus asked him if he wanted to be whole, he gave an excuse. He said no one would help him. One thing I learned is when Jesus asks you if you want something, there are only two involved. The one He is asking and the One who will ultimately answer. Jesus told the man to, "Rise, take up your bed and walk." Immediately the man was made whole and took up his bed and walked.

Things to note:

- *Sometimes you have to help yourself*
- *Don't be content with the attention you get from being "sick"*
- *Want it bad enough to talk to Jesus about it*
- *Don't make excuses for yourself*
- *Decide it is time to be whole!*

There may come a time that you may realize not only have you allowed yourself to go beyond the time needed to heal, but you may also realize the enemy has now taken advantage of your pain. Now it is more of a stronghold than a grieving process. It might take someone else to point this out, since we often are in denial about changes we may need to make. Especially when we started off with a legitimate reason for our pain. **But when God's word comes to you like they did to the sick man, decide you want to be made whole!** Allow God to give you instruction on what to do, and do it. He may have you reach out to someone else. He may have you do what you thought you couldn't do before. He may just remind you of the purpose you have had on the shelf for some time. But whatever God says for you to do – do it! His plan is that you be whole! Rise!

Father God,

Thank You for Your word that reminds me I am not a victim of my pain. I am not at a place that I cannot make decisions for my future and for my level of wholeness and sanity. Thank You for helping me realize I can choose to be healed and You will immediately begin the process in my heart and mind. I choose to hear Your word and hear from Your people that will help me. Help me remember the others around me that need my help to heal themselves. I am key to someone else's wholeness. I choose to be healed and to rise up every day knowing that I am empowered to conquer each day. Help me not to hold others accountable for how I recover from pain. I choose to take responsibility for myself and work through this time with You by my side. I give You praise for the days ahead. In Jesus' name. Amen.

Notes

CHAPTER 9

HEALING WITHOUT CLOSURE

How do you reach a level of healing when there is no closure to your pain?

Healing Without Closure

Examples of lack of closure

After the tragic attacks of 9/11, some of the thousands of people trying to go on with their lives found they had no bodies to bury. Even though people were pretty sure their loved ones died in the attacks, the nagging question still remains.

What can leave you with a lack of closure?

- ❖ A missing person
- ❖ Violent death with no one charged
- ❖ Hit and Run deaths
- ❖ A miscarriage or still birth child– unexplainable

What are some problems with lack of closure?

- ❖ You don't know, so questions stay in your mind
- ❖ There is no one to blame or to vent anger towards
- ❖ You are on a constant emotional string of hope versus despair
- ❖ Every day you seem to start the same process again

How do you heal without closure?

- ❖ Trust God with the unknown
- ❖ Don't feel guilty for trying to go on with your life
- ❖ Try to keep your mind from wandering
- ❖ Read and study scripture
- ❖ Keep your mind on God. He promises peace.
- ❖ Find people to help and encourage
- ❖ Don't allow the enemy to play with your mind

Philippians 4:6-8

"Be careful for nothing, but in everything with prayer and supplication with thanksgiving, let your requests be made known unto God. And the peace of God which passes all understanding, will keep your hearts and minds through Christ Jesus. Finally brethren, whatsoever things are true, whatsoever things are honest, whatsoever things are just, whatsoever things are pure, whatsoever things are lovely, whatsoever things are of good report, if there be any virtue, if there be any praise, think on these things."

God really knows all things. So even if you don't know, try to rest in the fact that HE does.

Father God,

Thank You for peace. Thank You for comfort. Thank You for being ever present and all knowing. I trust You with the unknown. For everything I want to know, for everything, I need to know, for every thing I may never know. I trust You. Lord You have never left me, even though I may feel that way sometimes. But when my emotions fight Your word, I choose Your word. I choose to believe that You care for me and my loved ones with an everlasting love. Everything I don't understand, I leave in Your hands. Touch my family and give us peace. In Jesus' name. Amen.

Notes

CHAPTER 10

WHEN UNBELIEVERS DIE

We have scripture that promises us God will save us and our households. Did He forget about our loved one?

When Unbelievers Die

One of the hardest things to deal with as a Christian is the death of a loved one that we believe is unsaved. The thought of our family or friends missing heaven is unbearable for believers. How do we go on when the question is nagging in the back of our minds? We have scripture that promises us God will save us and our households. Did He forget about our loved one?

Some things need to be put in God's hands and left there. We can guess, pray, hope and cry until we are without strength, but God holds eternity in <u>His hands</u>.

> And Jesus said to him, "Assuredly, I say to you, today you will be with Me in Paradise." (Luke 23:40-43)

The man on the cross next to Jesus was a murder and an unbeliever. Facing death caused him to have a talk with Jesus that not everyone heard. Some may have only known the life he led prior to his sentencing. But because of his last minute heart change, Jesus granted him a place with Him in paradise. Not everyone who dies has this conversation with God, but you don't know everyone that does. Trust God with the unknown. Don't try to push someone into heaven on hopes alone, but don't try to doom them to hell just based on the life you saw. Eternity is a choice each of us makes and we make it with God. He is the

only one who knows the end result.

Things to ponder:

- ❖ Unbelievers or believers alike, may have unconscious times when they cannot respond to you but are still aware. Continue to pray and read scripture to them. You never know what God is doing.
- ❖ Don't allow guilt over not witnessing enough to become an unbearable burden. The Bible still says, *"Some plant, some water, and God will give the increase."* You don't know who God had in their path before they died. (1 Corinthians 3:6-7)
- ❖ And finally, remember the last minutes of every person's life belong to God. He can touch, forgive, accept and change it all in a moment. It is in His hands. It is not His will that any perish, but that all come to repentance. He has done all that needs to be done to save our family and friends. But it will always be an individual decision.

Lord,

I trust You! I know that it is not Your will that any man or woman perish, but that all will come to repentance. So I leave all that I don't know, or what I don't understand, in Your hands. Father, help me to continue to be a light to people I come in contact with. Help me continue to care and share Your gospel message to the lost. By doing so, I may be the one that helps someone else's loved one come to know You. Help me hold onto the faith that says, if they confess with their mouth and believe in their hearts, You will save them. Thank You for the process of salvation. Though I may plant, another waters, and You will give the increase. Thank You for daily saving the lost. In Jesus' name. Amen.

Notes

CHAPTER 11

NOTABLE DEATHS

"Mourning for people we don't know, gives us an idea about who we are and what is important to us."

Notable Deaths

Do you know sometimes we can mourn for people we don't even know? We do it every day – A celebrity that we admired; a pastor outside our area whose ministry we received from; A mother or child in the paper; An innocent victim of a crime or disaster. We have the ability to be moved and hurt by the pain of others. What makes it notable is because we take note of it. It means something to us.

Think for a moment of people you didn't know, that you have genuinely mourned for. What was it about their death that made you mourn?

Was it:

- ❖ Someone you admired for serving our country, their talent or stance
- ❖ Things they achieved that was meaningful or helpful
- ❖ The numerous possibilities in their life that was lost
- ❖ The tragic or senseless way they left or those they left behind

> **Mourning for people we don't know, gives us an idea about who we are and what is important to us. It also gives us an idea of how much of God's heart we have grown to embrace.**

Death may cause us to realize that tomorrow is not promised to any of us. We may do more with our lives, live a little more focused on purpose. We may try to see dreams come to pass sooner, love our children more and prioritize our lives. Unfortunately, these changes can be short-lived and we may find ourselves falling back into the slump if we don't make the changes because of convictions instead of emotions.

Biblical Deaths We Remember:

- Elisha– His anointing continued even after he died
- John the Baptist– His life and death led people to Jesus
- Stephen– A martyr who died preaching Jesus
- Apostle Paul– his conversion and life is still a testimony
- Jesus– the purpose of His death is why we are saved today

"The memory of the righteous is blessed, but the name of the wicked shall rot" Proverbs 10:7

Father God,

I recognize that death is something that all of us will experience. Help me live my life in such a way that I bring glory to Your name. Help me lay aside every weight and sin that can entangle me daily, and live purposely for You. I appreciate each day You have given me, help me to treat others the way You would expect so when it is all said and done, I have impacted a life for Your glory. I love You and thank You that You are helping me keep things in perspective. In Jesus' name. Amen.

The end of your life should say, "I was here and God got the glory!"

Notes

CHAPTER 12

IT'S TIME!

"Take Courage, Give God Your Fears and Go Forward!"

It's Time!

Joshua 1:1-9

After the death of Moses, the servant of the Lord, it came to pass that the Lord spoke to Joshua the son of Nun, Moses' assistant, saying, "Moses My servant is dead.

 Now therefore, arise, go over this Jordan, you and all this people, to the land which I am giving to them--the children of Israel. Every place that the sole of your foot will tread upon I have given you, as I said to Moses. From the wilderness and this Lebanon as far as the great river, the River Euphrates, all the land of the Hittites, and to the Great Sea toward the going down of the sun, shall be your territory. No man shall be able to stand before you all the days of your life; as I was with Moses, so I will be with you. I will not leave you nor forsake you. Be strong and of good courage, for to this people you shall divide as an inheritance the land which I swore to their fathers to give them. Only be strong and very courageous, that you may observe to do according to all the law which Moses My servant commanded you; do not turn from it to the right hand or to the left, that you may prosper wherever you go. This Book of the Law shall not depart from your mouth, but you shall meditate in it day and night, that you may observe to do according to all that is written in it. For then you will make your way prosperous, and then you will have good success. **Have I not commanded you? Be strong and of good courage; do not be afraid, nor be dismayed, for the Lord your God is with you** wherever you go."

It is hard to imagine that God has purpose for us when we are in the midst of uncertainty. When things around us are messed up and our emotions are not exactly "spiritual." But God knew the loss you would encounter, even as He encouraged Joshua to release and go forward. He does the same for us. Moses was a leader and brother. He was a father and friend. But there came a time after his death that God said, "It is time to go on." It may not happen the first month or even the first year. But don't fool yourself. God still has plans for you. God has promised to be with you. He has promised to provide; to bring good success. Now it is time to trust Him. It is time to hear His word of comfort. Rise up and walk in it.

If you have gotten to the point that you know it is time:

Take a moment to:

- ❖ Look at your life
- ❖ Look at the promises of God
- ❖ Look at your goals
- ❖ Look at your possibilities
- ❖ Look at all those God still has for you to touch

Then Look at Your God!

Take courage, give God your fears and go forward!

Father God,

I am ready to hear Your voice speak to me. I am ready to take on strength and go forward. I know the path may be difficult, but You have always ordered my steps. You promised to never leave me or forsake me, so I trust You to hold me as I go forward. Thank You for caring so much for my future that You won't allow my past or present to hinder me. I choose to hold onto Your word and to allow Your people to help me as I go. I love You and thank You for hearing this prayer. In Jesus' name. Amen.

Notes

CHAPTER 13

PERSONAL NOTES

"Lord, I Thank You for Making Your Word Real to Me."

PERSONAL NOTES

It is sometimes easy to "encourage" people to do what you have not yet had to do. This book began as an assignment in 2003 to teach a class at my home church. I studied and prepared scripture and prayed for wisdom in how to deliver this message to many who were grieving and needing closure. It felt kind of hypocritical to teach and encourage people in an area that I had not personally experienced up close. But I am a teacher, and being instant in season and out of season is real to me. But one thing I understood was that God's word works, whether or not you have ever had to go through the many tests and trials that He provides deliverance for. You don't have to be a drug addict to have a word to help someone who is. You don't have to have been a prostitute to be able to encourage a young person in their worth. So although I knew and understood that I didn't have to lose someone in my family to make God's word work, it still felt strange continuing to minister to many in this area even though many said they were greatly blessed and helped.

On Veteran's Day November 11, 2009 both my very patriotic parents, Joe L Gunn (63) and Mary E Gunn (73), were diagnosed with cancer. On the same day! He had lymphoma and she had pancreatic cancer. For the next year they took turns undergoing major surgery, going to chemotherapy, radiation and being tested for a possible bone marrow transplant. There were hospital stays, ICU, trips to rehab centers and bouts with heart and knee issues. A lot of talks of lifestyle changes and later hospice then time to notify family.

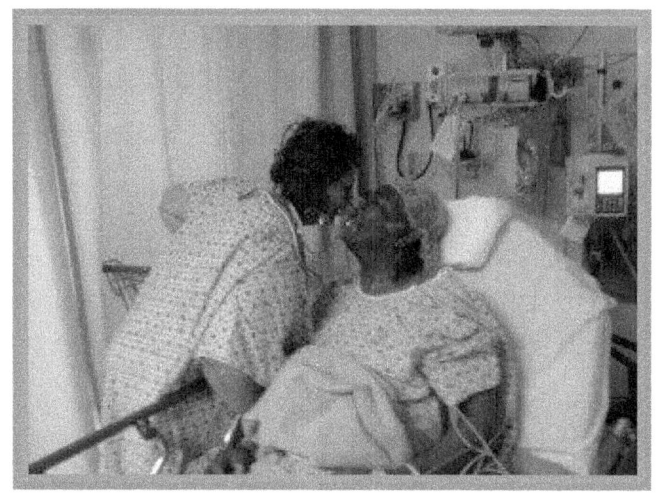

On June 24, 2011, DJ (Daddy Joe) passed away. Eight months later February 7, 2012, Mary (Mommy) passed away.

Death is a very real event in our lives. Even when we do all we know to do, pray all we know to pray and try all we know to try….It is still not our decision.

Here are a few things I learned and did, which helped me personally. I hope, like this book, it holds help for you too.

TRUST GOD'S TIMING

One thing I learned is to trust God. So much could have gone completely different if the timing was altered. The timing of their treatments and how there was never a time they were both in ICU. One of them was always doing better to help the other. If one was in the hospital, the other was visiting them. But somehow, we still saw

God's hand in everything. It was almost as if DJ planned how his wife would be taken care of. We, as his step children, have never been more proud of him than seeing how he cared for our mom, even in his death. We honor God in His timing, knowing that just as He held our parents, He also holds our future in His hands.

SHARING TASKS

It can be hard as adult siblings to share care. It can depend on work schedules, whether or not you have children or time. Just because someone seems to be single or have a lot of time, does not mean they have the grace. Our family was able to share responsibilities by setting up a conference call and talking about things that needed to be done. Not everyone was able to leave their family or travel. Not everyone was able to send finances. The key to making sure we share responsibilities is to know what everyone is able to do and not expect more than that. Some personalities are able to assist with baths or clean up after a rough night. But if someone is not able to handle that, allow them to do what they can do. Every need is important. Our mutual goal was our parents. Making sure they felt loved and cared for; not having them listen to adult children fuss with each other about someone "not doing their share." If someone in your family is doing the bulk of the care, just be sure you are doing what you CAN do. After all, it is for your loved one as well.

SORTING THINGS

I try to encourage people to never allow things to destroy a family bond. The best legacy you can leave for your loved one is the respect you have for each other in their absence. For us, distributing items was another huge task. After years of military living and travels, they accumulated years of stuff! Good stuff; memorable stuff. We implemented some simple guidelines: If one of the kids gave a gift within 10 years, that item went back to them to keep or give away. Some items were distributed based on who could care for it best or if they had room for it. The week we packed the house up, we coded the boxes by color for each sibling. That made it easier for the moving company as well as drops in 4 different locations from Houston, to Dallas to Tennessee.

One fun thing we did was when we distributed Mom's jewelry. We had a Jewelry Party! Since Mommy used to sell almost EVERYTHING! – Clothing, Tupperware, and jewelry – she had loads of jewelry. Not everything was expensive, but it was nice and definitely memorable since she was so stylish. So we had a jewelry party to distribute the jewels. Finger foods, soft music and Memory games were the agenda for the night. Each sister had to pull a card that said, "Share a Memory of …" with various times throughout our childhood, and "Pick 1 from Table 2" Or "Pick 2 from table 1". That is how we distributed the jewelry. Simple fun, memorable, and no reason for anyone to feel shunned. We finished with a turntable and old songs from the 60's-70'S. A few tears, but two lives well celebrated.

WHERE THERE IS A WILL…

I encourage everyone to look at doing a will before it is too late. If you have aging parents or even if you at a young age and have anything you can leave to anyone. Make it plain. By having a will it can eliminate a lot of issues. Even if someone does not agree with the will, at least there is a basis to begin. Be sure to keep your will current and update it as needed. Drawing a will does not mean you are about to die! It just means you are prepared if you do. With a family of 5, having both parents with a will was truly a blessing. We knew what they wanted, and were able to do it together. Having beneficiaries already listed for policies and bank accounts was another way to keep confusion down. We were able to pay outstanding credit cards because both my parents believed in insurance for their cards in the event of their death. So those cards basically paid for themselves. Take time to find out what steps you need to take to ensure your family has the right tools to function in the event of your death.

SO VERY GRATEFUL…

Overall, I must say, God has been good and faithful. You only bury your parents once. I am so grateful to God for His ever present help. We needed and still need Him. I am not sure how everyone handles the death of their parents, but now I know how I did. And I thank God that even though I miss them dearly, it is well with my soul.

A Final Thought...

This booklet was not intended to make light of your time of grief, nor was it intended to make you "hurry up" and grieve. The purpose is to let you know there really is life after death. And God holds both.

Reminders:

Even though you may be hurting or know someone who is, keep in mind that God has provided healing and comfort for us even now. He has given us people for our lives to help during hard times. They may not always know what to do, but the prayers of the righteous will avail. They will be there through the hard times, and the good times too.

Remember to grieve responsibly. No matter how much you hurt, try not to hurt others. Don't forget about those around you who are trying to help you – Your family, children, and friends. If we keep others on an emotional string, they run out of strength and stop coming around because we can be so draining. Others may feel insignificant in your life because you have no time for them and they can't help you. Know when it is no longer the grieving process that is hindering you, but the enemy who is using this occasion to beat you when you are down. Don't let yourself get that down. You can rise in the midst of pain and still be strong, even when it hurts.

Lastly, be encouraged! Know that we can handle more than we think we can, we can survive more than we think we can and when we feel weak, God has promised to be our strength and has graced us to endure. He is the God of all comfort and He promised to never leave us. (2 Corinthians 12:9-10)

~Jacqui Hill Goudeau

SCRIPTURE PROMISE

I Thessalonians 4:13-18

But I do not want you to be ignorant brethren, concerning those who have fallen asleep, lest you sorrow as others who have no hope. For if we believe that Jesus died and rose again, even so God will bring with Him those who sleep in Jesus. For we say to you by the word of the Lord, that we who are alive and remain until the coming of the Lord will by no means precede those who are asleep. For the Lord Himself will descend from heaven with a shout, with the voice of an archangel and with the trumpet of God. And the dead in Christ will rise first. Then we who are alive and remain shall be caught up together with them in the clouds to meet the Lord in the air. And thus we shall always be with the Lord.

Therefore comfort one another with these words.

ABOUT THE AUTHOR

Jacqui Hill Goudeau is an author, speaker, and blogger with a 30-year professional journey that spans a wide spectrum from retail, radio announcing, talk shows, to prison, children, and adult ministry. Friends consider her the ultimate storyteller. Her writings, to date, include *Embarrassing Faith*, *Getting the Lumps Out of Blended Families*, *Goudeau Gumbo for the Soul*, , a collection of poetry, *A Shoppers Guide to Dating* and *Departed Friends, Good Grief*, which addresses the issue of loss. Jacqui writes from her soul, making her books all-inclusive and easy reads for men and women, Christian and non-Christian alike. When you read her books, you immediately get a sense of wisdom that continues to be cultivated through life experiences, and most importantly, her intimate relationship with God. Just like an inspirational message, her books give you what you need, when you need it. Jacqui has a witty sense of humor, which people love. In her spare time, she loves gardening, painting, and watching movies with her family. You can contact her at www.wisdomspeakstoday.com for speaking info or other books

www.ingramcontent.com/pod-product-compliance
Lightning Source LLC
Chambersburg PA
CBHW070206100426
42743CB00013B/3077